Electricity

First published 2020
Foxton Books
London, UK

Copyright © Foxton Books, 2020

ISBN: 978-1-83925-007-1

Written by Nichola Tyrrell
Designed by Maryke Goldie
Logo design: Stewart Wright (2Wright Design)
Cover design: Ed White
Education consultant: Frances Barlow

About Foxton Primary Science:

The Foxton Primary Science series supports Key Stage 1, Lower Key Stage 2
and Upper Key Stage 2 Science.

This title supports the Electricity section of **Lower Key Stage 2** Science through a variety
of features and **STEAM**-inspired tasks that cover all curriculum requirements.

Colourful, engaging content blends information with prompts
for further discussion and investigation.

Keywords, creative activities and quizzes reinforce comprehension,
along with challenging words (in bold) explained in the glossary.

Contents

What is electricity?

Electricity is a form of **energy** that we use in all sorts of everyday objects. We use it for heating and lighting our homes, for kitchen appliances, computers and mobile phones, transportation and so much more.

Which items in this kitchen do you think need electricity to make them work?

There are two types of electricity: current and static.

Current electricity comes from batteries or from power points connected to mains electricity.

Batteries give power to objects such as a TV remote control.

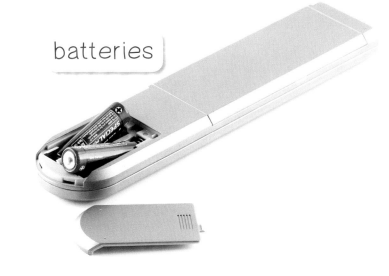

batteries

Some objects that need mains electricity have a plug. Others are connected to electrical wires in a building, like a light on a ceiling.

plug

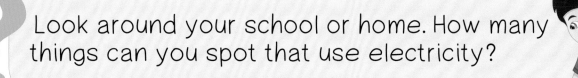

Look around your school or home. How many things can you spot that use electricity?

Static electricity is the build-up of electrical charge from friction, which can happen when you're going down a slide. Look at that hair!

5

Where does electricity come from?

Electricity is created in a power station using different types of fuel, or energy, such as natural gas, coal, oil, wind or **solar energy**.

Burning coal produces steam that can power a generator, a device that creates electrical energy in a power station.

Keywords fuel generator power

wind turbines

solar panels

Wind turbines and solar panels can also create energy to power a generator.

Electricity travels from the power station through wires to reach our homes, schools and other buildings. In the countryside, the wires are usually overground, linked by towers.

Lightning is natural electricity that is produced in thunderclouds.

underground wires

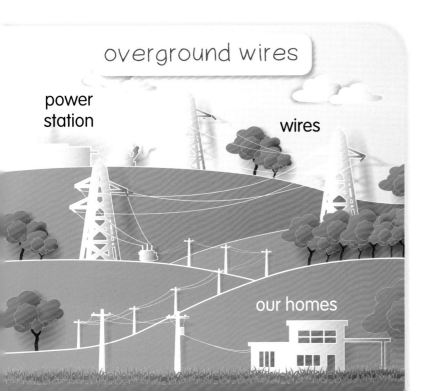

overground wires

power station

wires

our homes

In towns and cities, the wires are usually underground.

Electricity safety

Electricity can be dangerous. It is important to be careful around all sources of electricity. Think about the following safety tips and tell a grown-up if you notice any signs of unsafe electrical objects.

Keep water and wet hands away from electrical items.

Contact with a source of electricity can cause an **electric shock** or burn!

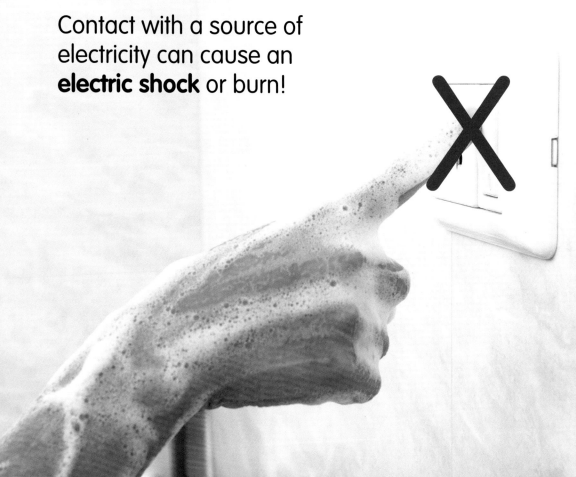

Keywords safety shock warning

Remove a plug correctly. Turn off the switch and don't pull it by the wire.

The big DON'TS:

- Don't put a metal object in a toaster.
- Don't fly a kite near a power line.
- Don't leave a mobile phone or other device plugged in and charging overnight.
- Don't put anything in a socket other than a plug.

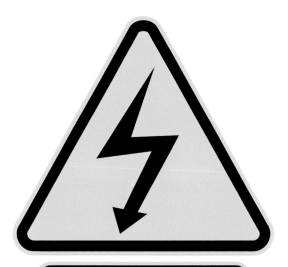

Always obey warning signs. If you see this one, stay away!

Tell a grown-up and STAY AWAY if:

- You see a broken wire.
- You see an overloaded power socket.

· WARNING ⚠ ·

DANGER ELECTRIC SHOCK RISK

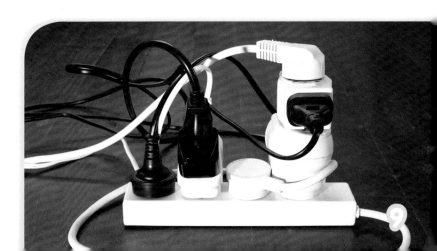

Finding electricity

Investigate your home to find items that use electricity. Record your findings and list which items use batteries or **mains** electricity.

mains electricity

batteries

or

You will need:
- observation chart and pen

Safety check

BE SAFE

While investigating your home, do a safety check for each appliance. Are any wires unbroken? Don't touch them! Are any electricals near a sink? Report either case to a grown-up. Turn to page 8 for a full list of safety tips.

Make an observation chart as follows:

Room	Battery	Mains
Electricity at home	Name: _____	
	Date: _____	
Living room		
Kitchen		
Bathroom		
Child's room		
Adult's room		

Which room in your home has the most electrical items?

Compare your findings with those of your classmates.

Think about what it would be like to live without electricity. Try an electricity-free evening at home with your family. How might you light a room, cook food or keep warm? How might you entertain yourselves?

Parts of a circuit

For an electrical object to work, it needs an electrical **circuit** through which the electricity can flow. The circuit needs certain parts that are connected to each other.

A light bulb will only light up if it is part of a circuit.

Keywords cell circuit motor switch wire

A working circuit must include:

a source of electricity (a battery, also known as a cell)

a switch to turn the circuit on and off

wires linking together all the parts

the object needing power

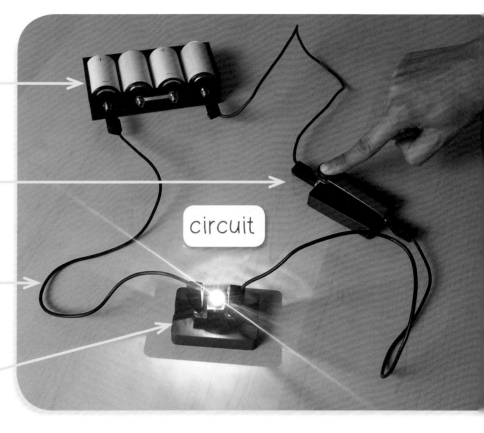

circuit

blender

A doorbell needs a circuit to make the buzzer ring.

Light bulbs are not the only objects powered by a simple circuit. A blender has a circuit to power the motor that makes the blades spin around.

doorbell

How a simple circuit works

A circuit allows electricity to flow out of a battery, through all the **components**, and then back to the battery. When the switch is turned on, the bulb, motor or buzzer will start working as electricity passes back into the battery.

There are many types of batteries.

Keywords battery negative positive terminal

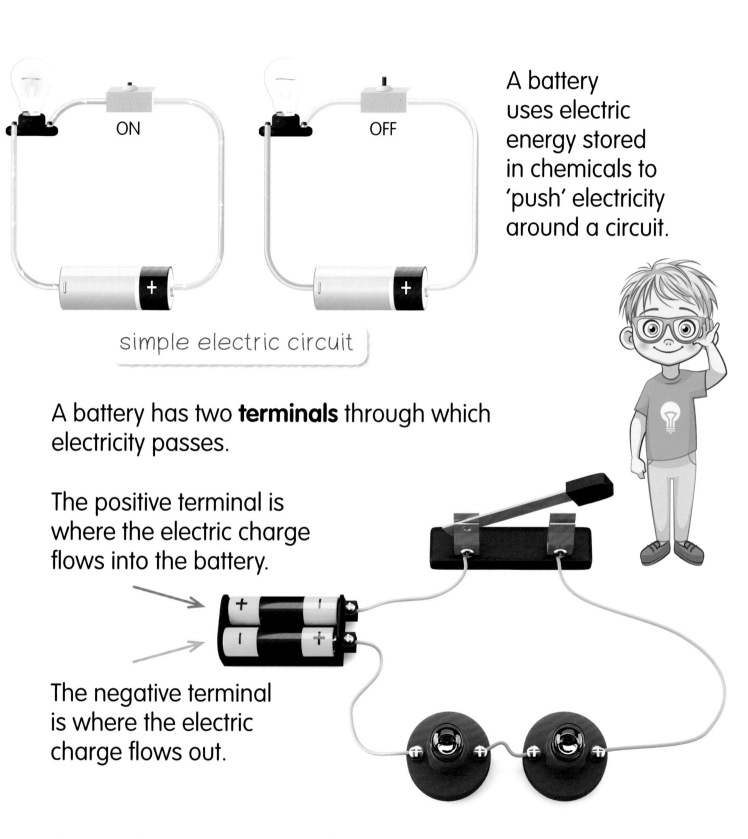

ON

OFF

A battery uses electric energy stored in chemicals to 'push' electricity around a circuit.

simple electric circuit

A battery has two **terminals** through which electricity passes.

The positive terminal is where the electric charge flows into the battery.

The negative terminal is where the electric charge flows out.

If a wire becomes detached, it causes a break in the circuit and the electric current will stop. Turning off the switch also breaks the circuit.

Changing circuits

We can increase or decrease electric power by making changes in the circuit. Make a lamp brighter or dimmer. Make a doorbell louder or quieter. Make a fan spin faster or slower.

Adding higher-voltage batteries to a circuit will increase power and make a bulb brighter.

Keywords   decrease   increase   voltage

Adding more batteries will also increase power. In a fan, the motor will spin faster.

a series circuit with two bulbs

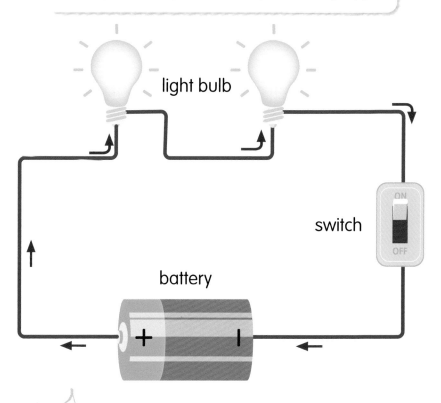

light bulb

switch

ON

OFF

battery

+ |

Adding more than one bulb to a circuit would make all the bulbs dimmer as each would receive less power. Several buzzers in a circuit would each sound quieter. Several motors would each turn more slowly.

Warning: too many batteries, or a battery with a voltage that is too high, will destroy a bulb!

Creating circuit diagrams

Draw a diagram of an electric circuit for a light bulb.

Remember to include all the components that a circuit needs and make sure they all join up.

Circuit components:

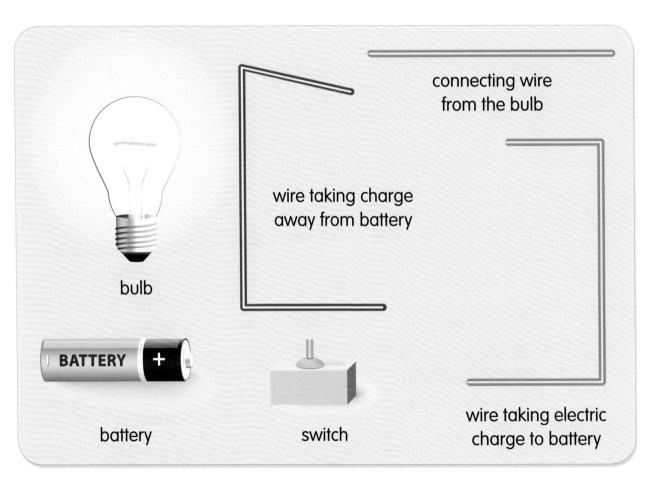

bulb

connecting wire from the bulb

wire taking charge away from battery

battery

switch

wire taking electric charge to battery

Now draw your circuit with changes.

Draw a bulb circuit that will make the light brighter.

Hint: there are two different ways to show this.

Draw a circuit with more than one bulb.

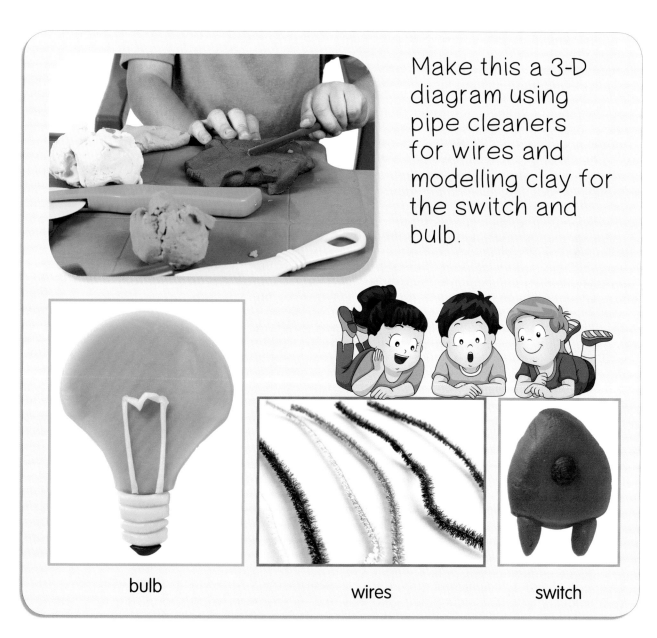

Make this a 3-D diagram using pipe cleaners for wires and modelling clay for the switch and bulb.

bulb   wires   switch

Conductors and insulators

An electrical conductor is a material that allows electricity to pass through it. It can link the positive and negative ends of a battery to create a circuit. An electrical insulator does not allow electricity to pass through it. We need both to build a safe working circuit.

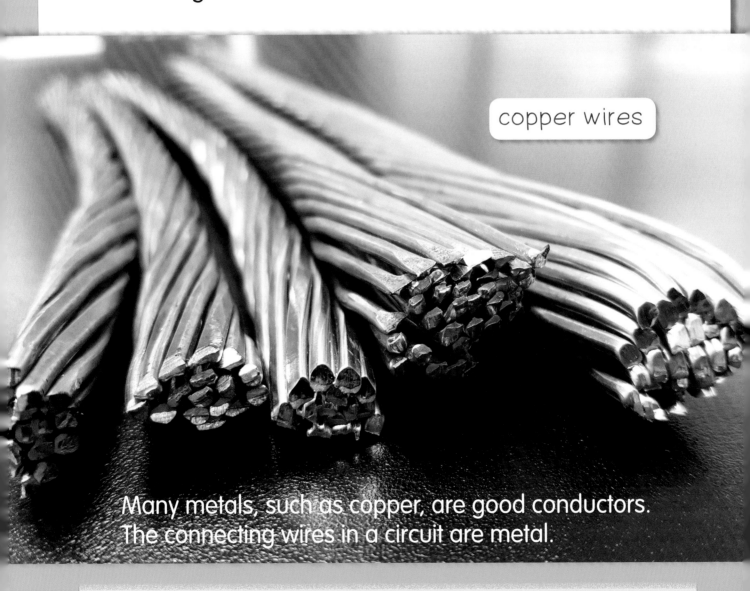

copper wires

Many metals, such as copper, are good conductors. The connecting wires in a circuit are metal.

Keywords   conductor   electric shock   insulator

The pins of a plug are metal so that electricity is easily passed from the wall socket into the plug's device, like a toaster.

The metal inside a light bulb, the **filament**, conducts electricity.

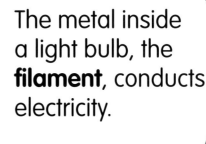

Plastic, rubber, glass and wood are good electrical insulators. They are used to cover conductors.

Connecting wires are covered in plastic to protect us from touching an electric current and getting an **electric shock**.

Electricians wear rubber gloves to protect their hands.

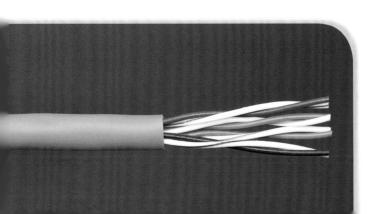

Building a circuit

Build an electrical circuit to light up a bulb. Start by making your own switch.

You will need:
- sheet of thick card
- 2 paper clips
- scissors

paper clips

thick card and scissors

Cut a rectangle-shape from the card measuring 6 × 3 centimetres.

Attach a paper clip to each end of the card.

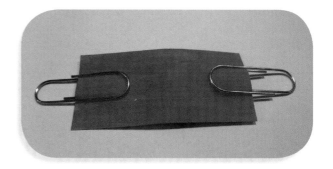

Your switch is now ready to add to a circuit by attaching crocodile clips (like the ones shown opposite) to each paper clip.

Now build a simple circuit and test it out. Connect all the components so an electric current can flow through.

You will need:
- a bulb in a bulb holder
- 3–4 connecting wires with crocodile clips
- batteries in a battery holder
- the switch you made

batteries in a battery holder

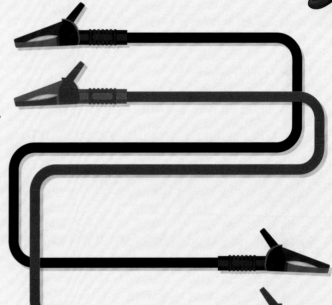

bulb in a bulb holder   connecting wires with crocodile clips

To turn on your switch, hold the connecting wires and fold the card so the paper clips touch – and watch the bulb light up!

Testing conductors

Investigate which objects are conductors and which are insulators.

You will need:
- a bulb and bulb holder
- 3 insulated wires with crocodile clips
- batteries
- 5 or more objects of different materials
- recording charts (see pages 26–27)

Ideas for objects to test:

nail or screw, eraser, plastic paper clip, pen, pencil, coin, scissors, sticky tape, spoon, tin foil

eraser

foil

spoon

sticky tape

pen and pencil

penny

1. Build an electrical circuit (see the previous page) but leave out the switch so the circuit is broken.

light bulb

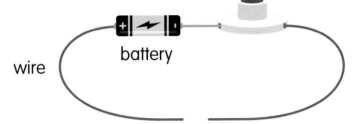

battery

wire

2. Choose one of the testing objects and predict whether it is a conductor or an insulator. Record your prediction.

3. Test the object by joining it to the components and completing the circuit. If the bulb lights up, the object is a conductor. If the bulb does not light up, it is an insulator.

Photocopy this chart or make your own:

Predictions and results

Name: _____

Date: _____

Object	Material	Prediction	Result:	
			Conductor	Insulator

What percentage of the materials tested are conductors?

Compare your materials. Were all the metal objects conductors? Did some conduct electricity better than others? What did the conductors have in common?

Copy this chart to organise your findings.

Conductor comparisons

Name: _____

Date: _____

Object	Material	Description	Type of conductor?	
			Strong	Weak

The strongest conductor is:

Comprehension check

1. What happens if a circuit has a break in it?

2. When connecting a circuit, does a battery need two wires or one?

3. Which component can break, or turn off, a circuit?

4. Does an insulator conduct electricity?

5. What are the two types of electricity?

6. Where is mains electricity created?

7. Is it safe to use an electrical item near water?

8. Is plastic a good conductor?

9. Is metal a good conductor?

10. Name three kitchen appliances that need electricity to work.

Turn to page 32 to mark your answers.

Vocabulary check

1. Electricity is a form of e _ _ _ _ _ that we use in all sorts of everyday objects.

2. For an electrical object to work, it needs an electrical c _ _ _ _ _ _ _ through which the electricity can flow.

3. Parts of a circuit are also known as c _ _ _ _ _ _ _ _ _ _ .

4. A battery has two t _ _ _ _ _ _ _ _ through which electricity passes.

5. An electrical c _ _ _ _ _ _ _ _ _ is a material that allows electricity to pass through it.

6. An electrical i _ _ _ _ _ _ _ _ _ is a material that does not allow electricity to pass through it.

7. The metal inside a light bulb conducts e _ _ _ _ _ _ _ _ _ _ _ .

8. Current electricity comes from a b _ _ _ _ _ _ _ or from a power point connected to mains electricity.

9. S _ _ _ _ _ _ electricity is the build-up of electrical charge from friction.

10. Natural gas, coal, oil, wind and solar energy are all types of f _ _ _ we can use to create electricity.

Turn to page 32 to mark your answers.

Glossary

Definitions relate to the context of word usage in this book.

appliance – a machine that uses electricity, such as a fridge

battery – the component of a circuit that is the source of power; it is also called a cell

bulb – the component of a circuit that will light up if the circuit is fully connected and switched on

buzzer – the component of a circuit that will make a noise if the circuit is fully connected and switched on

cell – the component of a circuit that is the source of power; it is also called a battery

circuit – a loop made of wire and components which electricity flows around

component – a part in an electrical circuit, such as a battery

conductor – a material through which electricity can flow, such as metal

crocodile clip – a metal clip at the end of a wire that attaches the wire to something else in the circuit

electric shock – the effect of electric current flowing through the body; it is painful and can be deadly

electricity – a form of energy

energy – the power to make something work

filament – the metal inside a light bulb

fuel – a substance that is burned as a source of energy

generator – a machine that produces electrical energy

insulator – a material through which electricity cannot flow, such as plastic

mains – electricity supplied to a building through wires

motor – the component of a circuit that will turn if the circuit is fully connected and switched on

negative – the terminal from which an electric charge flows out of a battery

positive – the terminal through which an electric charge flows into a battery

power – the ability to act or make something work

static – relating to electric charge within an object

switch – the component that turns a circuit 'on' and 'off'; it controls the flow of electricity around the circuit

terminal – the end of a battery that allows a connection to be made to an electrical circuit

voltage – the force of electric current measured in volts

wire – a thin strip of metal, usually covered in plastic, through which electricity can flow

Index

Quiz answers

Comprehension check, page 28

1. Electricity will not flow and the device won't work.
2. one wire 3. the switch
4. no 5. current and static
6. at a power station 7. no 8. no 9. yes
10. answers such as: fridge, oven, dishwasher, microwave, toaster, kettle

Vocabulary check, page 29

1. energy 2. circuit 3. components
4. terminals 5. conductor 6. insulator
7. electricity 8. battery 9. static 10. fuel

Photo credits

Shutterstock.com: pp 1–2: HappyPictures, Andrii Symonenko; pp 4–5: Joe Gough, Batanin, Erica Finstad, RTimages, lawang design; pp 6–7: Neil Mitchell, yuttana Contributor Studio, Soonthorn Wongsaita, theapflueger, Visual Generation; pp 8–9: Rad K, MPIX, Haryadi CH, Love the wind, yusufdemirci; pp 10–11: nazarovsergey, mariva2017, Vladimir Sukhachev, Helen Stebakov, Pallavi_Patil, Lano Lan; pp 12–13: U.J. Alexander, fen deneyim, Shebeko, Sarah Marchant; pp 14–15: Iren Moroz, Designua, haryigit, PinkPeng; pp 16–17: HappyAprilBoy, Tom Wang, Jakinnboaz, ONYXprj, Lorelyn Medina; pp 18–19: Designua, juninatt, Vectors bySkop, Seksun Guntanid, Lorelyn Medina, Robcartorres, GMEVIPHOTO; pp 20–21: beejung, Claudio Divizia, Francescomoufotografo, Ennie, Flegere, Victor Brave; pp 22–23: Tetyana Kozhemiakina, GraphicsRF, Dan Kosmayer, Lorelyn Medina, rumruay, haryigit, GrashAlex; pp 24–25: Lorelyn Medina, pirtuss, Irina Rogova, Pixelbliss, kongsky, yusufdemirci, Visual Generation, KK Tan; pp 26–27: Lorelyn Medina, Dualororua, Grishankov, AePatt Journey; pp 28–29: VectorPot; pp 30–32:GraphicsRF, Olkita, Lorelyn Medina, Teguh Mujiono

Pixabay.com: Cover: photoeightyeight; p 7: phillmarley; p 23: Conmongt; p 24: Hans